INDIE AUTHOR MAGAZINE

HELLO AND WELCOME!

I'm Indie Annie, and I'm thrilled you're reading this gorgeous full-color version of IAM. Did you know that you can also access all the information, education, and inspiration in our app? It's available on both the iOS App Store and Google Play. And for those that prefer to listen to me read articles, you can pop over to Spotify or our website. Happy Reading!

X

IndieAuthorMagazine.com

Download on the
App Store

GET IT ON
Google Play

Spotify

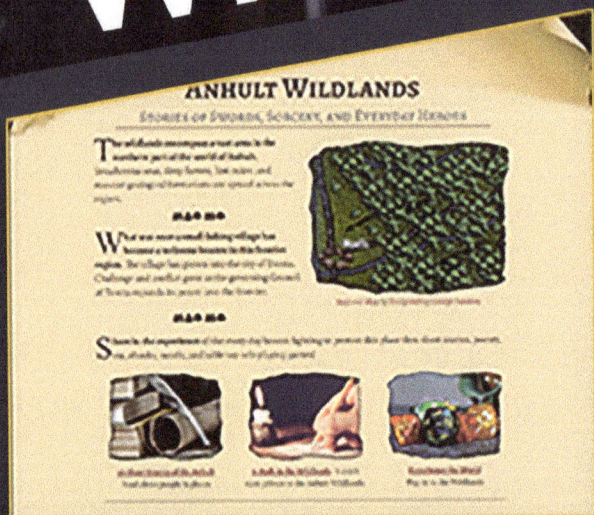

METADATA

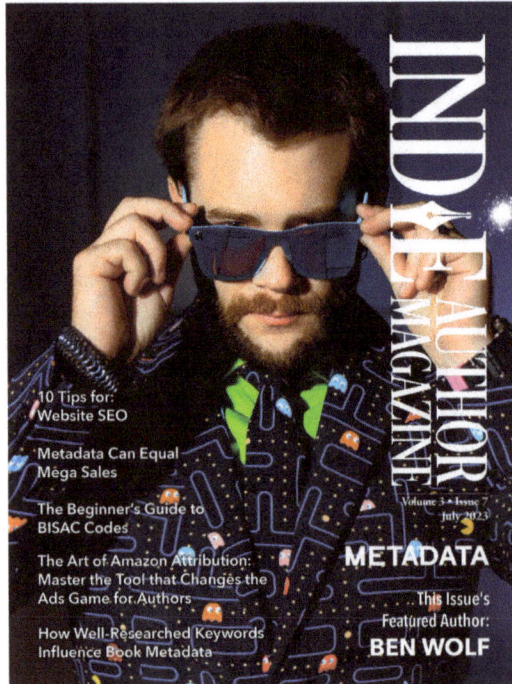

ON THE COVER

18   Unleashing the Imagination: Sci-Fi/ Fantasy Author Ben Wolf Conquers Dragons and the Literary World

14   10 Tips for: Website SEO

54   Metadata Can Equal Mega Sales

30   The Beginner's Guide to BISAC Codes

42   The Art of Amazon Attribution: Master the Tool that Changes the Ads Game for Authors

24   How Well-Researched Keywords Influence Book Metadata

REGULAR COLUMNS

12   Dear Indie Annie

14   10 Tips for: Website SEO

48   From the Stacks

THE WRITE LIFE

10   Martelle's Motivation

      Therapeutic Isolation

54   Prosperity

      Metadata Can Equal Mega Sales

60   Corner the Market

      Spend Money to Make Money

56   Mindset

      Journaling Tips for Authors to Preserve the Healing Power of Words

TYPEWRITER TALES

8   From the Editor in Chief

64   In This Issue

24
KEYWORD: DISCOVERABILITY

How Well-Researched Keywords Influence Book Metadata

30
THE BEGINNER'S GUIDE TO BISAC CODES

42
THE ART OF AMAZON ATTRIBUTION

Master the Tool that Changes the Ads Game for Authors

18
UNLEASHING THE IMAGINATION

Sci-Fi/Fantasy Author Ben Wolf Conquers Dragons and the Literary World

50
LOVE UNLEASHED, PG RATING GUARANTEED

A Guide to 'Clean,' or Sweet, Romance

36
DATA DRIVEN

How to Optimize Your Author Website with Google Analytics 4

INDIE
AUTHOR MAGAZINE

EDITORIAL

Publisher | Chelle Honiker

Editor in Chief | Nicole Schroeder

Creative Director | Alice Briggs

ADVERTISING & MARKETING

Inquiries | Steve Bremner
Steve@AtheniaCreative.com

Information
https://IndieAuthorMagazine.com/
advertising/

CONTRIBUTORS

Angela Archer, Elaine Bateman, Patricia Carr, Bradley Charbonneau, Honorée Corder, Jackie Dana, Heather Clement Davis, Jamie Davis, Laurel Decher, Fatima Fayez, Gill Fernley, Greg Fishbone, Jen B. Green, Jac Harmon, Marion Hermannsen, Steve Higgs, Chrishaun Keller-Hanna, Kasia Lasinska, Monica Leonelle, Jenn Lessmann, Megan Linski-Fox, Craig Martelle, Angie Martin, Merri Maywether Kevin McLaughlin, Lasairiona McMaster, Jenn Mitchell, Tanya Nellestein, Susan Odev, Eryka Parker, Tiffany Robinson, Clare Sager, Joe Solari

SUBSCRIPTIONS
https://indieauthormagazine.com/subscribe/

HOW TO READ
https://indieauthormagazine.com/how-to-read/

WHEN WRITING MEANS BUSINESS
IndieAuthorMagazine.com

Athenia Creative | 6820 Apus Dr., Sparks, NV, 89436 USA | 775.298.1925

ISSN 2768-7880 (online)–ISSN 2768-7872 (print)

Design like a Pro for free

FROM THE EDITOR IN CHIEF

Some of the best things about being an editor for *Indie Author Magazine* are the gems of wisdom I come across in our writers' stories.

Take Eryka Parker's feature on keywords in this month's issue. Like many of you, I'm sure, I've always viewed managing metadata as a bit of a chore—something we do to keep the algorithms fed and our books showing up in readers' search results. But Eryka's story approaches things from a new perspective: one that frames keywords as a way to build a relationship not with our distributors but directly with our readers.

It probably shouldn't be as novel a concept as it seems—or at least as it seemed to me when I read it. Everything we do as authors points back to our readers and lays valuable paths between us, especially marketing. The genres we select for our books are a promise of the kinds of stories we're going to tell and the story elements found within the pages. Why wouldn't our keywords be the same kind of promise?

Yet Eryka's perspective was an important reminder for me nonetheless. Metadata, at its most basic, is just a series of online breadcrumb trails leading readers—not distribution sites—back to our books.

None of this is to say crafting that metadata can't still pose a challenge. We've dedicated this entire issue to helping you make sense of it, in fact! But it's an interesting reminder of just why metadata is so important, and so deserving of its own *IAM* issue. On its own, metadata may just be a series of digital breadcrumbs. But if we only approach this vital step of publishing as a way to feed the algorithms, the path that's left may be too muddled to fulfill its true purpose: guiding potential readers home.

Nicole Schroeder
Editor in Chief
Indie Author Magazine

Therapeutic Isolation

Someone we like or respect is doing a thing. We want to be like what we admire. So we do the thing too. Often, that isn't healthy for us.

If something you're doing is causing you pain, then don't do it. If it's challenging you and making you uncomfortable, but it's helping you toward your goal, then don't quit. Either way, be honest with yourself. Is the thing you're doing just for social validation? Your friends are doing it, and if you want to spend time with your friends, then you need to do it too. Right?

I'd love for my wife to play golf, but she tried it and quickly abandoned it—for the right reasons. To do it right would take far more time than she was willing to commit, and that would've frustrated her. Perfect reasoning for a lifelong athlete.

If the thing you're doing is causing you pain and not challenging you as you strive for your goals, then why are you doing it? By all that's holy, stop seeking external validation when you'll never get what you want, and that'll bring you closer to your real goal.

We see authors jump on bandwagons that aren't aligned with their goals because the cool kids are doing it, or because someone else is making serious bank. But is that same thing going to fill your soul (and bank account)? Or is it going to suck the life from you for a short-term gain? If your heart isn't in your writing, the readers will know, and they won't be buying.

You can write to market—write with the reader in mind—and not leave yourself behind. Tweaking things to help a larger readership appreciate your book doesn't change the core message or your characters. The best stories are character driven. The other details are shades of gray.

Do you keep doing what your friends are doing? Or will you stay true to your goals? Keep your eye on the goal first, and invest your time in doing what it takes to reach that goal. Don't do what causes you pain and leaves you bobbing like a cork on a wind-blown lake.

That brings us back to therapeutic isolation. Sometimes, being alone to contemplate how you're doing is more important than joining the crowd and being swept away. What if the crowd is right and they're doing what you need to be doing? Then go in with your eyes wide open, and enjoy the ride. Friends who go a different way can still be friends, unless they demand you go with them when it doesn't help you get where you want to go.

Losing friends is no fun. Losing yourself is worse.

Stay true to your goals. Stay true to yourself. Sometimes it's good to be alone, but when you confidently walk your own path, you'll find others willing to join you. ■

Craig Martelle

Dear Indie Annie,

My last self-published book took off, and I'm finally gaining traction as an author. I'm eager to release my next book as soon as possible to keep the momentum going. But I need help to keep a regular writing schedule while also managing tons of promotional work. How can I stay productive and timely in getting my next book written?

Juggling in Jersey City

DEAR JUGGLING,

I understand the struggle to keep writing while promoting your first book! Publishing momentum is hard won but easily lost. However, with a few tricks and tremendous tenacity, you can tackle both writing and promotion.

First, treat writing time like a sacred obligation—non-negotiable blocks in your schedule, come hell or high water. Set a writing goal for each session: five hundred words, two pages, one good paragraph—anything to keep the draft moving. Even Hemingway had to sit his butt in the chair!

Establish a regular writing cadence, whether daily, weekly, or monthly. Stephen King famously writes two thousand words every morning to fuel his prolific output. Find a rhythm that works and stick to it.

Limit distractions during writing time by turning off notifications, closing tabs, and silencing your phone. Creating fiction demands an uninterrupted flow of ideas; outside "pings" break that flow. Take a page from J. K. Rowling's book and write your first drafts longhand, if needed, to minimize distractions.

On the promotion side, schedule social media in bulk, several tweets or posts in advance, rather than reacting to every ping. Pre-plan blog content for the month, and automate routine social tasks. The time you save not managing socials minute by minute can be devoted to writing instead.

Delegate other tasks wherever you can. Hire out some repetitive promotion tasks, or even invest in a part-time social media manager or publicist. The more tasks you remove from your plate, the more mental space and creativity you'll have for writing.

Need help from your favorite Indie Aunt?
Ask Dear Indie Annie a question at
IndieAnnie@indieauthormagazine.com

Remember, your words come first. If a promotional opportunity does not directly advance your next book, say no. Set boundaries that honor your writing as a sacred priority above all else. Toni Morrison famously wrote by hand with the curtains drawn for this very reason!

Join an accountability group or writing challenge to keep yourself on track. Maybe you could join millions of other authors in a writing challenge like November's annual National Novel Writing Month event. Many enthusiasts love collecting digital badges for their achievements. Personally, such organized communal jollity is my idea of hell. I would rather book a cabin in the woods and cut myself off from the world, preferably with a ready supply of cake, gin, and fruit mixers. A hot tub would sweeten the deal. The point is, my darling one, you need to find what works for you.

Once you have started, the most important thing is to trust the process. As Zora Neale Hurston said, "If you're in suspense as to completion, just keep on going, and the end will come right." Your fingers know the way, even if your mind gets lost along the road.

Sweetheart, whilst we all dream of being published and getting our precious baby out into the world, that's when the actual work begins. Ask any parent with more than one child: having the first was tough. It was terrifyingly new and exciting, with so much to learn. But baby number two changes the game all over again. You have to find time to do all you did with number one with the next child and still keep their older sibling alive. At times, it will seem impossible, and maybe you'll find that something has to give so you can cope. But ask parents with three, four, or more offspring, and they will assure you it gets easier. You will learn what is important. You will prioritize more effectively. You will establish processes that make your life easier. And you will find time to get your books washed and ready for bed every night.

Keep marching forward, my darling Juggling! Your next masterpiece and army of fans await—and the words are already within you. You just need to give yourself the space, schedule, and sacred stillness to let them flow freely onto the page.

Happy writing,
Indie Annie

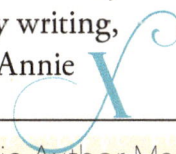

10 TIPS FOR
WEBSITE SEO

Search Engine Optimization (SEO) is the organic method of driving traffic to your website, as well as to your other channels. As opposed to targeting audiences with paid ads, SEO allows you to utilize keywords, content creation, and links to create meaningful metadata that will place your site in potential readers' search results and drive new audiences to your site.

Training Google and other internal search engines to connect potential readers to your site doesn't have to be complicated. With ten steps, you can boost your website to the number one spot on the first page of people's results pages. Since Google is the most used search engine, these ten tips will be Google-focused; however, you can use these tips across a great many platforms.

1 OPTIMIZE YOUR KEYWORDS

Keywords are vital for your brand to be discovered, but it's important to use relevant keywords in the right places, and not too many. Functional SEO requires that you start out with keywords that are relevant to your brand. What do you want your audiences to focus on? What marketing terms align with your product? Try writing a list of questions your intended audience might type when seeking your brand, and answer those questions. The best keywords are niched down so clearly that both Google and your audiences know you provide the value they seek.

2 CREATE KEYWORD-SATURATED CONTENT

To train Google's search engine, it is vital your website be filled to the brim with content. Why? All that content is keyword-heavy, and that is what Google likes. If your author website only has book covers and links to buy, it is too bare for Google—or your intended audience—to care about. Websites with great SEO have blogs, vlogs, podcasts, embedded social media, images, and more. Don't overdo it, but be sure there is enough content to engage your audience meaningfully for as long as you can.

3 LINK YOUR BRAND AROUND THE INTERNET

Links tell Google that your website gets around; the more people move in and out and all around your site, the more Google sees you as relevant and valuable. Link to your books, Pinterest, Facebook, Instagram, Twitter, or other social media. Link to any mention of your brand, such as book signings, events, and articles. Throw links in your blog posts. Make sure that each page of your website has a relevant link. What do I mean by relevant? Use links that have been clearly crafted with keywords in mind. For example, if you want to mention another author's book that you love, examine the keywords in the link to their page. Keywords like "romance-book-western-author-award" will do better at driving targeted traffic to your award-winning Western Romance brand than something like "huckleberry-OK Corral-Clint Eastwood-spaghetti."

Avoid linking your website to non-curated websites, not just for your SEO but also for optimal user experiences. When choosing links to use, send your audience to clean, well-respected sites with few ads. Every word you post on your brand's channels tells Google what to do. Do not confuse it with irrelevant links, no matter how interesting you think the article is.

4 GIVE YOUR AUDIENCE LOTS OF VIDEOS AND PICTURES

Google likes visual media along with keywords; the more pictures and video you can include, the longer your audience will linger, and the more your website trains Google its algorithms are working correctly. When posting videos, be sure to attach relevant keywords and metadata to connect your brand's content across sites. If you're using YouTube, the first hundred characters of your video's description need to lock in your viewer. Here are some tips for making that space count:

- Front load your description with a link to your website, and fill in the rest with a keyword-heavy video description.
- If your video is on the short side, add a full transcript in the description box or, for longer videos, a link to your website where you display the transcript.
- Use popular keywords relevant to your video as tags, but don't overdo it. Too many irrelevant keywords will distract Google from your goal.

Pro Tip: Taking steps toward a more accessible video can also help with your SEO. Create an SRT file to go with each video. This will add subtitles and captions, which will then become keywords in search engines.

Pictures and videos create visual interest, but they also carry keywords. File names themselves are perfect places to maximize SEO; instead of January-Vlog-Davis.mov, try something like Yourname-become-a-best-seller.mov. It might be Mount Saint Helens in the picture, but a great file label would include keywords that tell us why you are showing us the mountain and its relevance to your story. Don't forget to fill the image caption with keywords as well; Google sees everything.

5. CROSS-LINKING CREATES SEO DOMINANCE

Beyond linking to your site in other areas of the internet, cross-link everything within your website as well. Do you mention your first book on your About page? Link to it. If you are mentioning your design skills, link to your swag page. The goal, once you have your audience enveloped in the world of your brand, is to make them want to stay. Keep it comfortable to move around your world while making Google's web crawlers happy too.

Pro Tip: Keep in mind the marketing rule of seven: it will take seven impressions to make a click. Make those seven impressions so visually enticing people won't even realize how long they've stayed.

6. MAXIMIZE YOUR MOBILE CONTENT

When designing your website, examine how your website will show up on your audience's smartphone. Google uses a smartphone agent to crawl your website for information, specifically looking at it through the lens of a smartphone user. According to Google, "Make sure that your mobile site contains the same content as your desktop site." Often, mobile sites are streamlined and simplified, with just a few words and links. Since Google uses this mobile-first indexing, simplified versions with little content will not rank well enough for optimal SEO.

7. MAKE SOCIAL MEDIA WORK FOR YOU

Every Pinterest, Instagram, Facebook, and Twitter post you make should link to one or more of your website pages. Each of these channels has their own search engine as well. Utilize hashtags and keywords, but remember to keep them relevant to your brand. This means being intentional in the niche of your keywords; using irrelevant hashtags can distract the algorithms.

Pro Tip: It may be difficult to do, but being the first to create a specific branded hashtag can improve your SEO by allowing you ownership of the market.

8 MAKE GOOGLE SEARCH CONSOLE AND GOOGLE ANALYTICS YOUR FRIENDS

Once you have your website up and running, use Google Search Console to help you analyze your site's traffic and what keywords drove the audience to your content. Google Analytics gives you the tools to examine traffic to your website from all channels. Finally, Google Search Central provides an in-depth index for making all sorts of tweaks to your website to optimize SEO.

9 TURN YOUR WEBSITE INTO A THEME PARK

When building your website, try to create a world your audience never wants to leave. Entice them to read your blog post, then lead them to a podcast you made, a vlog on YouTube, your social media channels, your newsletter sign-up page, back to your website to buy the book they just learned about … Now you have optimized your SEO—and gained a fan.

10 FOCUS ON THE USER EXPERIENCE

According to Google, the search engine "rewards content that provides a good user experience." Clean, readable text on a secure website with easy navigation will go a long way to optimizing SEO. Think about your users' experience. For instance, focus on accessibility: dark background colors with light text are hard to read for some, so consider neutral background colors with black text, large navigation menus with commonplace words, and content designed for the mobile experience. Your goal is to make it to number one on Google's results page, but once you have your audience, it's up to you to keep them comfortable enough to engage. ■

Heather Clement Davis

Unleashing the Imagination

SCI-FI/FANTASY AUTHOR BEN WOLF CONQUERS DRAGONS AND THE LITERARY WORLD

Photos provided by Ben Wolf
Additional photo credits to Arpit Mehta

In the vast landscape of modern literature, there are authors who possess an uncanny ability to captivate readers with their words, whisking them away to worlds both real and imagined. Among them stands Ben Wolf, the award-winning author of multiple Children's and Middle Grade books, as well as the Blood Mercenaries Fantasy series and the Sci-Fi Horror series the Tech Ghost Trilogy.

Ben Wolf's origin story began with a remarkable event at the age of nine, when he slayed his first dragon—at least, that's how he tells the story on his website. As the dragon breathed its last, Ben writes, it imparted upon him the unique ability to lie creatively. The dragon's final words urged him to use this power wisely, and Ben embarked on a journey of discovery that ultimately led him to become the accomplished author he is today.

IN THE BEGINNING

Despite his early encounter with the creative, Ben didn't pursue his writing dreams straight away. "I went to school and studied for a four-year degree to be a pastor," Ben says. "I was working with youth and really enjoying it; however, the writing was always there, and I had story ideas that wouldn't leave me alone, and new ideas kept coming, and I realized I had to make a choice.

"It wasn't fair to the kids in the programs that I was working with when so much of my heart belonged to writing," he says. "So, ultimately, I made the very difficult choice to resign from my position and pursue writing, and I haven't looked back since."

It wasn't a journey Ben made alone. His wife, Charis Crowe, is also an independent author. They live in America's Midwest with their two children.

"We both took the plunge in the fall of 2017," Ben says. "I'd been rejected for the third time when I was right at the finish line with a traditional publisher. My book had gotten all the way through committee, and it made it to where just one or two people needed to say yes, but they didn't."

Inspired by indie success stories such as that of Shayne Silvers, and with a backlist of ten books, Ben decided to self-publish his work instead. "I figured 'I'm just going to take a shot and see what happens.' That was 2017, [and] here I am in 2023 with twenty-seven published works," he says.

LIGHTNING STRIKES

Of course, there's a little more to Ben's publishing journey than feeling the call and taking the plunge. A pivotal moment occurred in 2009, when he attended the American Chris-

tian Fiction Writers (ACFW) Conference—his first writing conference of any kind.

"That was when I learned that I was not as incredible as I thought I was," Ben says with a laugh. "I was very headstrong and thought just the fact that I can finish a book and make it action-packed and super fun … was going to be enough for publishers and agents to want me, and I had to be humbled in that regard."

The realization was one he now credits with getting him to where he is today. "After that conference, I realized there is so much about the craft of writing that I didn't know," he says. "I dedicated myself to reading books on craft, attending more writers' conferences, and putting it all into practice through some freelance editing and writing."

In 2009, Ben had only written one book, but he knew if he wanted to make a career out of

writing, he needed more. He set to work revising that first manuscript, which he is adamant will never see the light of day. But his second book did. He mastered the art of outlining after discovering that "pantsing" his way through each book did not end well, and he put his time and energy into developing the tools and skills he needed as a writer.

Part of that toolset was his skill as an editor. A self-confessed grammar fiend, Ben has carved a niche for himself as an editor and mentor for many other writers over the years. Back when he'd first made the commitment to his writing, he'd wanted to supplement his author income, preferably in the publishing field. Editing was the solution. "I've always been the type of person that couldn't necessarily tell you every rule grammatically that I'm following, but I inherently know what they are, and having studied as

part of learning the craft, I got better at it," he says. As his skills developed over time, he transitioned from editing for free to charging for his services.

Ben has also published a couple of craft books of his own, not to mention the craft blog he runs through his author website, https://benwolf.com, which is jam-packed with advice for writers at any level. It's perhaps little surprise that some of that advice emphasizes the importance of the editing process in bringing a book to life.

"No matter how good your manuscript is, it can be better," he says. "Find a good freelance editor who understands genre and understands the craft of storytelling, or if you're writing nonfiction, understand how to construct the type of nonfiction that you're doing. Not only will you walk away from that experience with a stronger manuscript, but you will have sharpened your tools for the next time you sit down to write a book."

Editing is just part of Ben's recipe for success. He also recommends authors ensure their books have an eye-catching cover and, most importantly, that they stick with the book until it's finished. "If your book isn't finished, you can't do anything with it," he says.

Beyond technical and craft skills, Ben says writers also have to have the courage to take the plunge and put their work into the world.

"I am a very risk-averse person, and I had to accept that … maybe if I'd started self-publishing some of the stuff that I had written earlier, I might have found more success online, just by virtue of being in the game sooner. I don't have a time machine—yet—so I can't go back and change it, but if you don't put your book out there when it's ready, then you're not going to advance your career or your dreams.

"Don't get in the way of your dreams; don't be the thing that keeps your dreams from coming true," he says.

THE NEXT ADVENTURE

Even with years of experience and several titles now out in the world, Ben's author adventure is still just getting started. After having undertaken a Kickstarter campaign a couple of months ago, Ben is currently preparing to launch his next Children's book, as well as another book that he co-authored with two friends.

He is also incredibly excited about an idea he came up with in 2014—one that he's taken on a nine-year development journey since. The project has taken more definitive shape over the last two years; Ben credits the connections he has made with the right people via the 20Books conferences in Las Vegas. The established Fantasy and Sci-Fi author is stepping into the world of GameLit, or LitRPG—short for Literary Role-Playing Game—to write additional content for the expanded audio edition of Dungeon Crawler Carl, in partnership with Soundbooth Theatre. These books are stories that involve gaming worlds and systems—the book version of watching someone play a video game. The book will be released this fall. "It's excellent training for me because I'm working closely with Matt Dinniman, who is, in my opinion, the best LitRPG author out there," Ben says.

This dragon slayer continues to conquer. ∎

Tanya Nellestein

Keyword: Discoverability

HOW WELL-RESEARCHED KEYWORDS INFLUENCE BOOK METADATA

Cracking the code of effective keyword use in book listings, book descriptions, and marketing can be intimidating. You need to be able to identify not only the language you believe describes your book but the language others may use to connect with it as well. Yet fine-tuning that language is an essential and ever-changing part of marketing your work.

Conducting market research and learning to think like your readers are valuable techniques for finding the right words to use. When it comes to applying them in your sales strategy, one of the most effective ways may also be one of the simplest: using those well-researched words, terms, and phrases to customize the keywords in your book's metadata.

UNDERSTANDING KEYWORDS AND METADATA

Mastering keyword and metadata customization takes time, effort, and energy. The two are closely related: keywords are specific terms or phrases that represent the main ideas, themes, or topics covered in a book, and metadata includes any other descriptive information about the book, such as the title, author, publisher, publication date, genre, and subject matter. Keywords are carefully selected to enhance a book's discoverability and aid in categorization. Metadata provides contextual information to help with cataloging, indexing, and retrieving a book from databases or libraries.

So it's easy—and correct—to conclude that keywords are an integral part of a book's metadata. Keywords aren't repeating information from the book's existing metadata. Instead, they provide additional information on related subject matter so readers and search algorithms can find the book based on specific topics or themes.

So how do you come up with them?

Nonfiction authors often use terms related to their book's focus; if a book is about reiki, its metadata might include keywords such as "energy healing," "mindfulness," "holistic," and "seven chakras." Fiction authors may use keywords aligned with themes, tropes, and subgenres in their stories. The simplest place to start may be to make a list of twenty common terms or phrases your reader would use in an online search for your book. Then expand the list with synonyms. Before you know it, you'll have a list of forty or fifty words to interchange.

Speaking of interchanging keywords, it's good practice to update your keywords every once in a while; doing so will grab your readers' attention and make your book more discoverable by search engines. Be mindful of any buzzworthy trends related to your topic or theme. Sprinkling in a few of them along with evergreen terms—more common terms for your theme or topic, such as genre keywords—will balance your content to appeal to a diverse range of markets.

These are basic principles of keywords, but the tools can be more impactful than authors may realize—and there are plenty more ways to generate them effectively to market your work.

USING KEYWORDS FOR RELATIONSHIP BUILDING

Every author seeks to understand what their audience wants in a story. The key to intriguing readers into purchasing your book is establishing a connection with them. Keywords, even as a basic marketing tool, can help spark that connection.

A primary step in the relationship-building process is identifying the themes in your book that your readers are most interested in. Knowing the solution your book provides, your readers' needs, and how to fulfill their expectations of a particular genre will help you craft a strong author brand—and find the keywords that resonate with them the most.

To start, consider how your readers most commonly find their book titles.

- **Word of Mouth:** Recommendations from librarians, friends, family, or colleagues are a powerful and trusted way for readers to discover new books that often carry significant weight.

- **Online Reviews:** Readers often turn to online platforms such as Goodreads, Amazon, book blogs, or social media platforms to read reviews, observe ratings, and gather recommendations from fellow readers and other trusted sources.

- **Bestseller Lists:** Bestseller lists provide a curated selection of popular and trending new titles and authors that are receiving significant attention and acclaim.

- **Bookstores and Libraries:** Browsing these physical and online platforms remains a classic way for readers to explore curated displays and discover catchy titles and new genres.

- **Author Events and Literary Festivals:** Book signings and literary festivals provide opportunities for readers to receive personalized book recommendations.

- **Book Clubs and Reading Communities:** These social settings provide book discussions and shared recommendations that introduce readers to new or trending titles that may be out of their norm.
- **Book Awards and Literary Prizes:** Prestigious book awards and literary prize nominations, shortlists, and winners are often highlighted in media coverage or book promotions.
- **Online Book Retailers and Algorithms:** Online retailers like Amazon frequently use book recommendation algorithms based on shoppers' browsing history, purchase patterns, and customer reviews.
- **Book Blogs and Influencers:** Book bloggers, BookTubers, and social media influencers who specialize in book recommendations in specific genres can significantly impact readers' book selections because of their trusted opinions and ability to discover new books.

Study the themes, topics, and keywords used by your readers' trusted sources and in the comments of their followers, and you can begin to identify which words will resonate most with your target audience—and put your book in front of them. Pay attention to online book recommendation requests of friends who read in your genre, as well as the keywords their followers use to recommend titles. This data, along with the previously mentioned sources, can be valuable content for your book listings and metadata.

GENERATING KEYWORDS: COMPETITIVE TITLES AND SEO TOOLS

You're likely already familiar with the central themes, topics, or subject matter of your book, but will readers focus on different aspects of it when describing your work? When generating keywords, take on your readers' perspective and include specific words and phrases they may use to describe your book or books like it. According to IngramSpark, "The more specific the keywords, the more likely the person searching for those specific words will be happy to find your book among the search results."

It may be tempting to use generic or overly broad keywords to try to attract a larger audience, but terms like these won't guarantee your book shows up for potential readers with the most interest in your work. Identify a targeted audience to increase engagement with your book.

Next, study which keywords your book's competitive titles used in their book listings and marketing. Similar books in your genre can provide insight and inspiration for refreshing your keyword bank.

Another option is to leverage research keyword tools and platforms for fresh keyword suggestions. Using these tools can help keep you informed about keyword popularity and broaden your selection.

Google Ads (formerly Google AdWords Keyword Planner): Besides ad campaign support, Google Ads can provide insight into search volume and keyword suggestions based on your book's topic or genre.

Amazon SEO: When publishing a book on Amazon, this platform offers keyword suggestions based on your book's title, category, and description to help you optimize your book's metadata and product listing for better visibility within Amazon's search results to connect with more readers.

BookBub: This platform offers book marketing and promotion as well as blogs and resources on book marketing strategies, such as keyword research and optimization.

Keyword.io: This free longtail keyword research tool collects keywords on specific topics from various sources, including search engines and platforms like Amazon, Google, YouTube, Bing, Fiverr, and more. Some of its features include Google autocomplete, Amazon autocomplete, and Fiverr autocomplete.

Google Trends: Google Trends allows you to explore the popularity and search volume of specific keywords over time and can help identify trending or seasonally relevant keywords for your book marketing efforts.

These resources are starting points for your keyword research, and the results can be adapted specifically for your book and target audience.

PERIODICALLY TEST AND REFINE YOUR KEYWORD LIST

Lastly, it's important to monitor your book's performance and adjust your strategy accordingly. Continually update and optimize your keyword selection to improve your book's discoverability.

Be sure to evaluate keyword effectiveness over time. Your book's sales performance, as well as its position in your search results, will help you determine if you're on the right track. And if a particular keyword isn't yielding the results you want, don't be afraid to swap it out.

Choosing effective keywords requires a healthy balance between specificity and popularity. Aim for keywords that accurately represent your book's content and are relevant to your target audience's search habits, and you can't go wrong. ∎

Eryka Parker

The Beginner's Guide to BISAC Codes

Over the years, we've seen adaptations in how books have been categorized. The changes have been prompted by libraries, publishers, and bookstores and were put in place to make it easier for booksellers and readers to navigate the extensive, ever-growing catalog of books available.

Think about walking into a bookstore and wanting to find a book. In this scenario, this is one of those spectacular two-level bookstores with shelves of wonderful tomes. Where do you go to find the book you want?

In the late 1980s, the Book Industry Study Group (BISG) developed a hierarchy to foster efficiency in the book industry and help brick-and-mortar stores and online retailers categorize books based on their content. The classification system is called the Book Industry Standards and Communications code, or BISAC for short. As a school media specialist-librarian, I like to think of the BISAC system as the business world's adaptation of the Dewey Decimal System. Thanks to these codes, ask for a book, and any bookstore employee will likely be able to walk you directly to the shelf where it's stored, along with similar stories to the one you're looking for.

With the BISAC system, every book category is given a nine-digit alphanumeric code. This is where I'd like to point out that keywords are not BISAC

categories. Keywords are terms readers use to identify a specific book or trope and cover a broader variety of topics. Amazon's categories can also be separate from the BISAC system—for instance, "Fantasy TV, Movie & Game Tie-In" is a searchable term and category on Amazon but is not listed as a BISAC subject heading. The BISAC Subject Heading list uses a limited list of specific categories that is standardized in the North American book industry.

In that humongous bookstore from earlier, the fiction and nonfiction selections are likely separated. The adult section is separate from the children's section, and the teen section has another little area in the store. Within those areas, the topics branch out into further subcategories. You can find the complete list with links to subcategories at https://bisg.org/complete-bisac-subject-headings-list. That is the beauty of the BISAC system. It is consistent, making it easier for booksellers to place books and for readers to find them.

WHY DO BISAC CODES MATTER?

Using the BISAC system to organize bookstores and other distribution sites is more than just an aesthetic choice. Without the BISAC system, title organization could vary from one place to the next, and a book could easily end up in the wrong category because, often, a category has both fiction and nonfiction classifications. "Marriage and family" may be a subcategory under the nonfiction category Family and Relationships, but it is also a subcategory of Fiction, Humor, Juvenile Fiction, and YA Fiction. A reader could want a book with practical advice on how families can manage their busy lifestyles, but without a system in place, they could be misdirected to a book about a zany family that learns to appreciate each other through the highs and lows of day-to-day life.

This is just one topic. Think of books on King Arthur. Is the reader looking for a retelling, a story inspired by the historical time period, or factual evidence of the original story? BISAC codes ensure they get the book closest to meeting their needs.

HOW DO DISTRIBUTORS USE THEM?

The BISAC system is widely used by various retailers in the book industry, but it isn't just another optional marketing tool.

For these distributors and others, it's a required piece of your book's metadata. Here are some major retailers and platforms that catalog books using BISAC codes:

1. Amazon uses BISAC codes extensively to organize books on its platform. In the past, authors could ask to have books added to as many as ten categories, but as of June 2023, this has changed. The updates to how authors use the Amazon categorization system mirror other retailers' systems, helping readers find books that suit their interests. In the book detail section, authors choose up to three categories as listed in the BISAC Subject Heading list. The search terms they'd like associated with their books go into the keyword section but do not guarantee the book will be listed in the categories associated with the terms.

2. Barnes & Noble, a prominent bookstore chain in the United States, also employs BISAC codes to classify books in its physical stores and online platform. Authors can apply up to three codes per book. This allows customers to browse books by specific subjects or genres. It is also why a reader can walk into any store and find what they need; the layout is similar.

3. Many independent bookstores utilize BISAC codes to categorize their inventory and make it easier for customers to browse and discover books of interest within specific subject areas.

4. Various online platforms and book distributors, such as Ingram, Baker & Taylor, Google Books, and Kobo, rely on BISAC codes to classify and organize books within their catalogs. Users can search and explore books by subject, making it more convenient to find relevant titles.

BISAC CATEGORIES

ANTIQUES & COLLECTIBLES	LITERARY COLLECTIONS
ARCHITECTURE	LITERARY CRITICISM
ART	MATHEMATICS
BIBLES	MEDICAL
BIOGRAPHY & AUTOBIOGRAPHY	MUSIC
BODY, MIND & SPIRIT	NATURE
BUSINESS & ECONOMICS	PERFORMING ARTS
COMICS & GRAPHIC NOVELS	PETS
COMPUTERS	PHILOSOPHY
COOKING	PHOTOGRAPHY
CRAFTS & HOBBIES	POETRY
DESIGN	POLITICAL SCIENCE
DRAMA	PSYCHOLOGY
EDUCATION	REFERENCE
FAMILY & RELATIONSHIPS	RELIGION
FICTION	SCIENCE
FOREIGN LANGUAGE STUDY	SELF-HELP
GAMES & ACTIVITIES	SOCIAL SCIENCE
GARDENING	SPORTS & RECREATION
HEALTH & FITNESS	STUDY AIDS
HISTORY	TECHNOLOGY & ENGINEERING
HOUSE & HOME	TRANSPORTATION
HUMOR	TRAVEL
JUVENILE FICTION	TRUE CRIME
JUVENILE NONFICTION	YOUNG ADULT FICTION
LANGUAGE ARTS & DISCIPLINES	YOUNG ADULT NONFICTION
LAW	

The beauty of the consistency of the BISAC system is that any reader can explore from one site or bookstore to the next without having to adapt their research methods.

SELECTING BISAC CODES FOR BOOKS THAT DON'T FIT THE MOLD

Selecting the right BISAC categories can be easier for some authors than for others. If your book blurs genre lines or doesn't seem to fit neatly into certain categories, it can take time to figure out where your book fits best—but there are ways to make it easier.

When publishing a book on Amazon, authors select BISAC code options from a drop-down menu that mirrors the BISAC listings on the BISG site. After choosing a category, authors can then select more specific subcategories from an additional list. If you're not sure where yours fits, here's a great author hack: find books similar to the one you are adding to your KDP Dashboard and read through the categories they use. Tools such as Publisher Rocket (https://publisherrocket.com) and K-lytics' genre reports can also help when reviewing the options.

Other online retailers, such as Barnes & Noble, Draft2Digital, and Google Books, have a search function that helps the author find the best-fit book categories. In the search bar, type the book category or subcategory. From there, the system suggests a list of options to choose from. When I searched Horror, I received four suggestions. Thriller garnered fourteen possible listings.

Still need to niche down? Add additional search terms or tags to the metadata. For

instance, you can categorize a book as Fiction-Romance-Later In Life, but in the keywords section, you can also add terms like "second-chance romance," "dating," or "best friend romance" to more accurately describe your story.

The BISAC system is a living document, and the BISG is aware of the ever-evolving nature of the book industry. The organization reviews and updates the subject headings list annually, and on their book category page, BISG provides a link to a form for authors to offer suggestions. Bear in mind, several examples of books that fall within the suggestion are required to validate the request.

HOW TO MANAGE BOOKS FOR READERS AGED 18+

Beyond categories for story content, the BISAC system also has a hierarchical organization that indicates whether a book is appropriate for readers under eighteen. The YA and Juvenile categories say the book is suited for readers under eighteen. Anything outside those categories indicates the material may not be suitable for younger readers because of language or subject matter in the story.

Choosing the appropriate BISAC codes won't limit how your story appears in searches and may

in fact help more of the right readers find your story. Moreover, indicating when a book has explicit content is working under the guidelines of best practices of the BISG. By not doing so, the author—and by default, the bookseller—risks attracting readers that would take offense.

The beauty of the BISAC system is that major categories and subcategories make it easy for a publisher to indicate wether the material contains explicit content. For instance, Horror is a category for dark elements. Several main categories have Erotica listed as a subcategory.

Online retailers have also taken measures to ensure the right reader finds the right book.

Some outright have a checkbox that asks, "Is this material unsuitable for someone under the age of 18?" If the answer is yes, they will then ask if the material is erotic or explicit.

As long as authors answer these questions truthfully, distributors can ensure the book is shelved or coded in the correct section of the store.

Remember, the BISAC system is not meant to eliminate publishing options or confuse authors. Experiment with the options and research categories to find the best fit, and you'll make it easier for the right readers to find your book. ■

Merri Maywether

Data Driven

HOW TO OPTIMIZE YOUR AUTHOR WEBSITE WITH GOOGLE ANALYTICS 4

Your author website is gorgeous. I mean it. It is aesthetically pleasing, consistent with your branding, and customized to guide your readers on an effortless journey from discovery to superfan.

But does it work?

You've spent a lot of time, when you could have been writing, thinking about how to reach your readers, engage them, and keep them coming back. Now you're staring at your subscriber list, social media followers, or bank account, wondering if any of the cool things you offered found the people who want them.

You could keep watching all those dashboards and guessing which of your actions affected them, or you could use a web analytics service to compile data that tells you exactly what you want to know about your readers and how they use your site.

Analytics tools measure data like the number of unique visitors to your site, the duration of their sessions, their search queries, response to ads, and purchase conversions. Understanding this data is essential for making decisions that will boost your website's goal conversion rate, whether you want the site to sell your books, connect readers to a fan community, or collect email addresses for your newsletter.

A few of the metrics most analytics services review include:

- **Your Audience:** Find out where they come from, what language they speak, and which devices they prefer, and use that data to make informed decisions about your website, your brand, and maybe even your writing. Are you reaching your ideal reader? Do the readers you are reaching want or need something you aren't yet providing (like translations, or serialized stories optimized for mobile reading)?
- **Traffic Sources:** How are your readers finding you? Are the ads you use worth the money? Did you find any new readers through that giveaway? Do people make the jump from social media to your website?
- **Activity:** If your website has multiple pages, are people clicking through? Do they stay on your blog long enough to read your content? Are they finding your newsletter landing page?
- **Conversions:** Do people sign up for your newsletter? Are they downloading your reader magnet? If you sell direct, which products are they buying? Maybe it's time to look into merchandising.

WEB ANALYTICS SERVICES

The most popular web analytics tool is Google Analytics. According to a survey by W3Techs, "Google Analytics is used by 86.0% of all the websites whose traffic analysis tool we know. This is 56.5% of all websites." Alternative tools like Clicky, Mixpanel, Piwik, Plausible, Kissmetrics, and Woopra offer many of the same features and may provide a less intimidating user experience, though none of them provides the range, depth, or customization of Google Analytics, and most come at much higher price points since the standard Google Analytics is free.

Pro Tip: In July 2020, Jin Wang of Jin & Co. (https://jinand.co) looked at the secret statistics of successful author websites. His blog post provides more tips for authors looking to make the most out of the data they collect with Google Analytics.

WHAT IS GOOGLE ANALYTICS?

According to its website, Google Analytics "is an analytics service that enables you to measure traffic and engagement across your websites and apps." The newest version of the platform, Google Analytics 4 (GA4), came out of beta in October 2020 and replaced Universal Analytics (UA), Google's previous analytics platform, as of July 1. The most notable difference between Universal Analytics and GA4 is in how the properties collect and process data. While UA grouped data by sessions (user interactions within a given time frame), GA4 collects interactions based on events, including page views, button clicks, and other consumer actions. This model is designed to make Analytics more flexible, more scalable, and faster, as customers move away from independent sessions on desktops in favor of cross-platform experiences with apps. The change also better complies with new data protection regulations.

Pro Tip: Analyzing analytics and want to learn more? Check out Skillshop's series of courses developed by Google to introduce their products, or AgencyAnalytics' blog article on the program (https://agencyanalytics.com/blog/what-is-google-analytics-4). The website is geared toward marketers, so it's an accessible introduction for authors without a background in web development.

FEATURES

Besides gathering data on website usage and conversion metrics, GA4 offers several new features to help you manage information.

Customized Dashboards
Edit the default dashboard to suit your needs and style. Use templates, or build your own and select which metrics to track.

Add custom widgets to determine how each data set is displayed: as a numeric representation, timeline, geomap, table, pie chart, or bar graph.

Some widgets update automatically in real time, and others update when you refresh or load the dashboard. Widgets can also be linked to specified reports, filtered to exclude certain data, and segmented into groups for comparison.

Built-In Automation
GA4 uses machine learning to enhance traditional tools like the search box. In addition to searching for specific reports, insights, and help content, you can now ask a range of questions about your data and get immediate answers. As with any artificial intelligence interface, the more specific you can be about the metric, dimension, and time frame you request, the more likely you are to get the desired response.

Additional new capabilities include

- Automatic alerts by email or text for trends in the data, such as increased demand for a specific product, or a sudden drop in traffic that may indicate a problem with the site,
- Calculated churn probability that can help anticipate customer actions, and
- Other predictive metrics, such as revenue estimates from audience groups.

Reporting and Explorations
The updated property simplifies the previous list of predefined reports by giving you a few overviews that can be expanded for deeper insights. "Summary reports" give a high-level snapshot of insights like how users found your business and which parts of the business are engaging them most. "Realtime reports" allow you to monitor activity as it happens to show you how readers are currently interacting with your platform.

Using a new section called "Life Cycle," you can track customers throughout a marketing funnel and receive reports on acquisition, engagement, monetization, and retention.

If those don't get detailed enough for you, the new Explore section allows you to customize the way you analyze data. Using a drag-and-drop feature in Explorations, you can select only the metrics you're interested in and filter, segment, or sort them as you choose. GA4 offers templates for six different techniques, but you can also create your own.

As the creator, you determine who can view or edit your explorations. If you choose to collaborate, you can share your explorations and view explorations that other users share with you.

Data Collection and Management

Instead of relying on cookies to gather data on your site's users, GA4 properties use a combination of identity spaces, including device ID, user ID, and Google signals, to create more accurate reports when users interact across multiple devices. This shift from depending on cookies relies more on data modeling to fill in the gaps and allows you to identify unique users no matter what platform they use, which can help you determine the effectiveness of your marketing campaigns across platforms.

Integrations

Through GA4's integration with Google ads, you can now see in-app and web conversions for Google Ads; YouTube Ads; non-Google paid channels, such as Facebook; and organic channels, including search, social, and email. This allows you to monitor and compare various ad streams to ensure your marketing investments make sense.

Analytics also works with other Google solutions and partner products, like Ads 360, Display & Video 360, Google Cloud, Ad Manager, Google Play, and Google Search Console, many of which were previously only available at the enterprise-level Google Analytics 360.

Pro Tip: If you've been using Google's Universal Analytics, some of these features may be new to you. Bernard May discussed the four things you need to know about the changes for GA4 in a March 2023 article for *Forbes*. And if you aren't sure how to move to GA4 without losing data you've already collected in UA, Matthew Guey created a Writer's Guide to Google Analytics 4 at Reproof.app to help writers make the switch before UA goes away.

PRICING

GA4 comes in two forms: Standard (free) and 360 (paid). The biggest difference is in the amount of data each version can handle. The standard version covers five hundred events per user per day and retains data up to fourteen months, so it's more than enough for authors running a sole proprietorship or LLC, and other small to midsize businesses.

GA4 360, the corporate variant, comes with enterprise-level support, including a dedicated account manager, and is designed for large businesses who regularly see traffic above 1 million visitors per month. Its pricing is usage based but starts around $50,000 a year.

GETTING STARTED

You can access GA4 tools by creating an account directly through Google or by using a Wordpress plug-in to connect it directly to your site. Once you have your dashboard set up, you can automate scheduled reports, track e-commerce if your shop is linked to your author website, set goals, and customize alerts. You can even set up multiple dashboards to monitor different data, like website traffic, social media and digital marketing results, and page views and keyword performance. If these options feel a little overwhelming, Google provides a ten-minute video walkthrough of the new GA4 interface to help you find your way around.

Your author website needs to support your business without distracting you from the real work of a writing career. Using the data provided by a web analytics service allows you to make your site more efficient, so you can spend more time writing the stories your readers love. ∎

Jenn Lessmann

The Art of Amazon Attribution

MASTER THE TOOL THAT CHANGES THE ADS GAME FOR AUTHORS

Imagine creating a captivating Facebook Ad for your latest novel. It garners attention, driving traffic to your book's Amazon page. Then comes the million-dollar question: how do you calculate the impact of this ad? How many clickers turn into customers?

Advertising is a key part of any author's marketing strategy, capable of turning the unknown into a household name. But for ads to bring about the best results, understanding and optimizing their performance is critical. For the longest time, tracking whether ads on other platforms led to sales on Amazon was a guessing game. That changed with the expansion of the Amazon Attribution tool, previously only available to third party sellers but now available to Kindle Direct Publishing users as of September 2022.

This powerful tool is free and accessible on the Amazon Ads dashboard, and it doesn't require an author to run Amazon Ads in order to use it. So what does it actually do? Amazon Attribution creates links that allow you to track sales and page reads from individual ad sources. Connect them to ads on Facebook, BookBub, emails, and on other platforms, and you'll be able to monitor the data associated with each ad source individually.

For authors, this tool is transformative, providing you with the information you need to adjust your strategy in real time. It paves the way for smarter decisions, better ad optimization, and, ultimately, more book sales.

THE GAME-CHANGING ATTRIBUTES OF AMAZON ATTRIBUTION

Before September 2022, KDP sellers didn't have a way to confirm that a click on a Facebook Ad directly led to sales or page reads on Amazon. With Amazon Attribution, that—and a host of other benefits—are available.

For one, with the tool, authors now have access to conversion reporting. No more guessing games about which ad campaigns translate to sales or page reads; authors can log in to the console and access reports at their convenience or schedule them at specific intervals. This allows for quick decisions that optimize ads during campaigns, ensuring you get the most out of your advertising spend.

Amazon Attribution also has cross-platform tracking capabilities. It can unify performance data from multiple ads across different platforms, providing a comprehensive overview of your ads and how they've each affected Amazon sales and page reads.

SETTING UP AMAZON ATTRIBUTION: A STEP-BY-STEP GUIDE

Now that you understand the "why" behind Amazon Attribution, let's delve into the "how."

Author Nickolas Erik provides a detailed overview of how authors can set up the tool on his website: https://nicholaserik.com. Below, we've included some of his tips for setting up Amazon Attribution to track your book ads.

1. **Navigate to the Amazon Ads dashboard:** Go to the Amazon Ads dashboard and find the Amazon Attribution section under "Measurement and Reporting." Ensure you're in the Amazon Ad dashboard region where your ad will be running.

2. **Create a new campaign:** Click on "Create Campaign" to generate links for a new book or ad platform. You can then choose between manually creating a campaign or uploading a file for a bulk import.

Measure your non-Amazon marketing activities

Set up Amazon Attribution measurement for your non-Amazon campaigns across channels such as email, social media, paid search, display, influencer and affiliate marketing, and owned tactics that link to Amazon (ex. brand website, blog posts)

Learn how to get started

Create Campaign   Dismiss

3. **Add your advertised book to the campaign:** When setting up a campaign, add only the advertised book instead of your entire series or catalog. This makes it easier to get an accurate snapshot of how many sales and reads your ads are generating for that specific book.

4. **Use a clean link to build the attribution link:** Use a clean Amazon link, free of extra parameters, to create the attribution link. According to Erik, you should avoid using redirect services or link shorteners like bit.ly; instead, use the attribution link directly.

5. **Create unique attribution links for each different ad:** Each ad you run should have a unique attribution link. This enables you to compare the performance of different ads, helping you optimize your ad budget by identifying high and low performers.

Create ad group

Add ad groups and specify platforms and channels where your campaign is running on.

Ad group 1   ...

Ad group name	AI Issue - Facebook	Enter a name for the unique attribution tag you are creating.
Publisher ⓘ	Facebook ⌄	Choose the website, app, or other property where your media will be displayed.
Channel ⓘ	Social ⌄	The ad type (for example Display, Video, Social, Search, or Email).
Click-through URL ⓘ	https://www.amazon.com/Magazine-Special-F(	Enter the destination URL when a user clicks your ad, email or social media post.

6. **Align the attribution link name with the ad's name on the ad platform:** Match the names in Amazon Attribution to the names you're using on the ads platforms to keep data from each ad campaign separate and easy to analyze later.

Campaigns ⓘ	Ad group ⓘ	Publisher ⓘ	Channel ⓘ	Attribution tags ⓘ	Click-through URL ⓘ
Indie Author Magazine - AI Issue 5778068712048641B0	AI Issue - Facebook	Facebook	Social	https://www.amazon.com/Magazine-Special-Featuring-Artificial-Intelligence/dp/1957118164?maas=maas_adg_2B9668C0C11BA3548E702E7CB7CD6CDB_afap_abs&ref_=aa_ma	https://www.amazon.com/Magazine-Special-Featuring-Artificial-Intelligence/dp/1957118164

DECODING AMAZON ATTRIBUTION METRICS

Now that you've set up Amazon Attribution, you'll start gathering valuable data about your ads. But how do you interpret this information to make informed decisions? Here are some things to keep in mind as you review your attribution data to guide your ad optimization:

1. **Last touch attribution model:** This model attributes sales and reads to the most recently clicked ad when a potential reader clicks on multiple tracking links. Understanding this model will help you better assess the direct impact of individual ads on your sales.

2. **Fourteen-day attribution window:** Users must buy or read a book in the two-week period after clicking an attribution link in order to count on the dashboard. Understanding this window helps you grasp the typical timeframe between ad engagement and sales.

3. **Data accuracy:** In his post from February 2023, Nikolas Erik reported discrepancies of 10 percent to 15 percent in Amazon's dashboard reporting and that of the traffic source (e.g., the Facebook Ads dashboard, BookBub Ads, your email service provider, etc.) and wrote that it is normal. Keep this in mind when comparing data across platforms.

4. **Reporting lag:** Data recorded with Amazon Attribution doesn't sync in real time and instead updates a few times a day. It takes about eight to twelve hours for clicks to show up; other metrics like detailed page views, sales, and reads come in gradually over the next twenty-four to forty-eight hours. Consider this lag when you plan to review your data for the most accurate insights.

OPTIMIZING YOUR AD CAMPAIGNS WITH AMAZON ATTRIBUTION

Once you have your Amazon Attribution set up and key metrics decoded, it's time to take your advertising strategy to the next level. Consider the following methods of analyzing the data you record to improve your campaigns:

Identify High-Performing Ads: Use your Amazon Attribution data to identify which ads are driving the most sales and reads, and allocate more of your ad budget to these successful campaigns.

Discard Underperforming Ads: Similarly, identify ads that aren't yielding a satisfactory return on investment (ROI). Consider discontinuing these ads to prevent wasting your budget.

Experiment with Different Ad Creatives: Since Amazon Attribution allows you to create unique tracking links for different ad creatives, test and compare ad versions using different links to examine which gets the most buzz.

Adjust Your Advertising Based on the Fourteen-Day Attribution Window: If you notice that most of your conversions are happening within a few days of clicking the ad, consider running shorter, more intensive campaigns.

Overall, Amazon Attribution can be an indispensable tool for authors in the digital age. Understanding how it works, setting it up, and interpreting the data it generates can be the key to a successful, data-driven ad strategy. ∎

Chelle Honiker

Hey You!

Why Isn't Your Ad Here?

From the Stacks

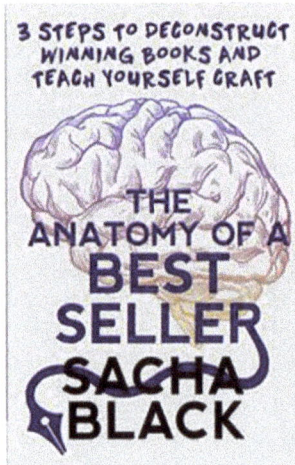

The Anatomy of a Best Seller: 3 Steps to Deconstruct Winning Books and Teach Yourself Craft (Better Writers)
Sacha Black

The Anatomy of a Best-Seller by Sacha Black is an engaging guide for aspiring authors aiming to understand the craft of best-selling books. This comprehensive guide provides a step-by-step process for deconstructing your favorite books, allowing you to understand and employ the tools of successful authors. The book offers tips and tricks for breaking down everything from sentence-level prose to plot, pacing, characters, and story arcs, and offers an in-depth guide to understanding your market and reader preferences.
https://books2read.com/u/m2qyqk

Indie Author Tools—Relaunched

Indie Author Tools is about to take a giant leap forward! Relaunching on July 1, this dynamic resource hub for self-published authors will unveil a sweeping redesign and expansion, featuring over three hundred new tools. From writing apps and marketing websites to courses and events, Indie Author Tools is the go-to source for everything an indie author needs to succeed. Renowned as the imagination's toolbox, this site is dedicated to empowering authors on their journey, whether they're crafting their debut novel or managing a growing book empire. What's more, it boasts a vibrant community where authors share reviews and guides, ensuring an unbiased, practical perspective on every tool. Don't miss the relaunch; your journey to literary success is about to get a whole lot easier with Indie Author Tools!
https://indieauthortools.com

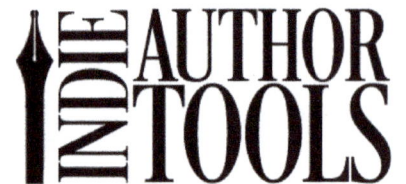

Indie Author Magazine—Full Audio Versions

Tune into the Indie Author Magazine Podcast, where the written word meets the spoken word! This unique podcast presents full audio versions of each month's issue articles from Indie Author Magazine. Perfect for busy authors on the go, each episode transforms insightful articles into engaging audio, allowing you to keep up with the latest industry trends, writing tips, and author interviews, wherever you are. Whether you're at your writing desk, commuting, or taking a well-deserved break, the Indie Author Magazine Podcast ensures you never miss a beat in the self-publishing world. It's not just a podcast; it's a community of authors sharing, learning, and growing together. Tune in to hear diverse voices from the indie author realm and fuel your author journey with wisdom from peers and experts alike.
https://podcasters.spotify.com/pod/show/indieauthormagazine

Love Unleashed, PG Rating Guaranteed

A GUIDE TO 'CLEAN,' OR SWEET, ROMANCE

In 2022, the Romance genre generated nearly one and a half billion dollars in sales, making it the highest-earning genre in fiction. It was also the fastest-growing fiction genre, contributing to 66 percent of adult fiction growth, according to statistics shared by data research group WordsRated (https://words-rated.com/romance-novel-sales-statistics/). Clearly, people love to read about love.

The good news is that the audience is vast for authors in the Romance genre. It can be difficult, however, to understand which subgenre your writing style falls into and how to reach those readers best. Clean Romance, often also called Wholesome or Sweet Romance, has increased in popularity over the last several years, and in 2016, Amazon introduced its Clean & Wholesome Romance category, which in itself became a roaring success. But as the subgenre has grown, so too has the controversy surrounding it and what belongs—or doesn't belong—in the category.

Like "spicy" or "steamy" descriptions, clean stories can mean various things to various people. Readers, reviewers, and authors in various genres have used the term to mean no cursing, no violence, or no sex scenes, but the range of what this looks like can be daunting. Fortunately, there are a few steadfast rules surrounding the Romance genre, and no matter how much authors debate how stories should be labeled, reader expectations are the ultimate yardstick by which a Romance author should measure their story.

So where do you draw the line in order for something to be labeled "clean"? What do readers expect, and how can you, as an author, meet those expectations? Are there resources for marketing "clean" books that might help attract the proper audience to your stories?

THE IMPORTANCE OF LABELS (NO MATTER HOW MUCH WE HATE THEM!)

There is a large debate in the author world about the implications of labeling certain fiction as "clean," but regardless of where you stand, readers looking for a particular type of book may have the final say. Until books have a universal rating system like TV or movies, categorizing stories within the immense genre of Romance comes down to using categories or labels that target readers recognize, such as Contemporary Christian Romance, Religious Romance, and Clean & Wholesome Romance.

Many books are also recently adopting the "Sweet" Romance label, which seems to carry a slightly different meaning than those labeled "Clean." This classification encompasses stories where romance is light and bedroom scenes fade to black. Readers often refer to Sweet Romance as clean, innocent, wholesome, or "rated G," in reference to film rating standards of the Motion Picture Association of America. But "Clean" Romance is often solidly rated G whereas "Sweet" seems to have a little more leeway and drift into a PG rating. This simply means that readers of stories labeled "clean" may expect no heat whatsoever, but readers of stories labeled "sweet" may be more accepting of small doses of on-page affection. Language can also be a significant consideration for stories labeled clean, sweet, or wholesome. Most readers in these categories do not want to see swearing of any kind—it's almost as important a requirement for some as the romance angle.

BALANCING READER EXPECTATIONS WITH CREATIVE WRITING

In an ideal world, the Romance genre would have a rating system comparable to TV or movie ratings with a list anyone can access. (I remember when TV ratings were initially improvised. It made television viewing so much easier!) The time may come when book ratings are standardized, but for now, authors have the difficult task of managing and meeting their readers' expectations.

Sweet or Clean Romance has virtually no limit to the storyline, so you can write about cowboys, billionaires, geeks, the guy or gal next door, paranormal or fantasy themes, historical romance, romantic comedy, and so on. As long as the relationship develops without readers watching what happens behind closed doors, you can don the label of "clean" or "sweet." And while the debate among authors about labels and meaning in "Clean" Romance is hot, the agreement among genre readers is strong that the stories shouldn't be.

KNOW THY READER

The key to success as an author is to know who your readers are, what they expect or want, and how to give them stories that keep turning pages and putting dollars in your pocket. To this end, book promotion sites and reader reviews can provide valuable information.

Book promotion sites have two goals: to gain new subscribers, and to keep those subscribers happy so authors will spend money to advertise to them. Whether you use a promotion site, their guidelines for marketing to readers can help you understand what your ideal readers may look for. Below are a few sites that market to Romance readers; though people have differing views about how much steam to play with, these sites can be helpful thanks to the fairly specific content guidelines they provide for authors in each subgenre.

- The Fussy Librarian: https://thefussylibrarian.com/advertising/about-the-content-ratings
- Full Hearts Romance: https://fullheartsromance.com/heat-description
- Rated Reads: https://ratedreads.com
- My Book Cave: https://mybookcave.com/mybookratings

K-lytics' 2023 Clean & Wholesome Romance market report also includes data and information on the subgenre and its expectations. The report is $37 and can be purchased at https://k-lytics.com/clean-romance.

Ultimately, the requirements for a book to fit the "clean," "sweet" or "clean and wholesome" labels are mostly straightforward. If you aren't finding happy readers or feel the level of physical intimacy, language, or other aspects of your story push the envelope, consider listing your title in a different subgenre, and be specific in your blurb about the level of spice or steam laid across the pages. The beauty of publishing in today's digital marketplace is that you're free to explore what works for you and your style, and you'll find readers who love you for it. ■

Tiffany Robinson

Metadata Can Equal Mega Sales

Get a handle on your book's metadata, and you can turn your book into a veritable cash machine. Ignore the finer points of metadata, and your book might fail to find the traction, impact, and income you would really like it to have. That would be a bummer.

For those of you who cringe, as I do, when you hear words like metadata—or just data, period—you're not alone. Our brains want to focus on things that are fun and do those things that are easy. If data doesn't come easily to you, you might pretend it doesn't exist. That would be to your, and your book's, peril.

There are plenty of articles in this issue about the intricacies and details of metadata. My job in this article is to help you with your metadata money mindset.

Let's start with this: you can do hard things.

You've already done about a zillion really hard things and come through with flying colors.

Did you graduate high school, and then maybe college? Did you get an advanced degree? Run a marathon? Travel abroad? Learn a foreign language? Buy a house or car on your own? Interview for a job? Become a parent? Move—maybe more than twice?

Yes, maybe you've done some or all of these hard things, or maybe you've done others. At the very least, you've written a book, and that's a feat on its own!

You're also smart enough to be a writer, and you're curious enough to read this magazine and this article. You can learn the ins and outs of metadata and how to maximize them for your book over time as long as you dedicate yourself to it.

Of course, that may sound easier said than done. But as with most things I don't find fun or easy, I've developed some hacks for getting from point A to point B while enjoying the process—or at least not hating it.

Step One: Find a metadata mentor. My buddy and coauthor, Brian Meeks, loves data. He's wicked smart and can explain complex concepts in an easy-to-understand way. Find someone in your life like Brian, and ask them to simplify the parts of the concept you don't understand.

Step Two: Learn one thing at a time. Just as you didn't learn how to craft your stories all in the same day, you don't need to learn everything about metadata before supper. The best place to start is at the beginning, so start there!

Step Three: Make it easy to feel successful. Every time you read an article, apply a new strategy, or have an aha moment, have a cookie. Our brains love a good reward, and proving to yourself you can do something, combined with a cookie, is a recipe for success. You know it's true—you love to do things that make you feel like you've made progress. The cookie is just an added bit of magic.

Step Four: Stay at it until you can do it on autopilot. For each thing I learn, I do my best to teach it to someone else, so it sticks with me. I want to learn it until I know it, and use it until it becomes second nature.

You'll get the hang of finding the correct title, subtitle, keywords, categories, and more. The more you'll do it, the better you'll get at it. Guess what? That means you'll make more of an impact—and therefore more of an income. See how it all comes together? You've got this. I believe in you!

Here's to you and your book's success! ■

Honorée Corder

Journaling Tips for Authors to Preserve the Healing Power of Words

Now that we're more than six months in, can you say you charged into this year replenished and ready?

With a barrage of external stressors, including political divisiveness, inflation, weather-related tragedies, and health concerns, it would be easy to guess that affirmative answers to that question are low. Compound that with the flurry of life and the struggle in recent years to find a "new normal" following the COVID-19 pandemic, and it is no surprise that stress and burnout are at all-time highs, according to the American Psychological Association. The world, especially in the last couple of years, has given us an array of challenges, and many of us are struggling.

But we have options.

Exercise, particularly yoga and stretching, can be good for writers who often sit in one place for long periods of time. You can choose to connect with friends, read a book, adjust your diet, meditate, laugh, or hug a pet, according to Mayo Clinic. There are plenty of options, but one in particular may seem targeted to writers especially: journaling.

WHY JOURNAL?

Journaling and its more structured cousin, therapeutic or expressive writing, have a long history. Many famous visionaries have been vocal about their journaling habits: several world-renowned scientists and artists, such as Marie Curie, Albert Einstein, Thomas Edison, and Leonardo da Vinci, practiced journaling, as did writers Anais Nin, Ray Bradbury, Oscar Wilde, Virginia Woolf, Sylvia Plath, and Anne Frank.

"When I write I can shake off all my cares. My sorrow disappears, my spirits are revived!"
-Anne Frank, The Diary of a Young Girl

Psychologists recommend journaling as a way to notice and manage anxiety symptoms, reduce stress, gain distance from traumatic experiences and cope with mental health challenges, and to embrace the opportunity for self-talk, or focusing on your own inner voice. Therapeutic journaling can also be used as a treatment for a variety of diagnoses, according to the US Department of Veterans Affairs (VA), ranging from the physical, such as different cancers, to the psychological, such as post-traumatic stress disorder. And the opportunities it can provide are diverse: releasing negativity, exploring themes about which you are curious, recording inspiration, creating a symptom diary, working through affirmations, analyzing recurring themes, and more. For writers, journaling can also offer a chance to warm up one's inspiration, to brainstorm ideas, and to play with words without an audience. We can use our creativity and love for words for ourselves, with only our own judgment to worry about.

HOW TO JOURNAL

Journaling is not the same as traditional writing. Although it can take many forms, it has a different format and purpose than the creative writing we do as authors. Methods for journaling range widely from structured formats, like preprinted sheets and dated prompts, to something more free-flowing. Some people have even taken to just scrawling squiggles as they think about what to write instead of actually writing the words. Julia Cameron's Morning Pages method from her book *The Artist's Way* consists of writing three pages of stream-of-consciousness thoughts upon waking every day. Other options include bullet journaling, often shortened to bujo; free writing; prompts; a gratitude journal; or a project-specific journal.

Searching for details on any of these can net you hours of beautiful journals and a great deal of inspiration. Of course, there is no right way to journal. The process differs for everyone, and experimentation is part of the process. The best kind of journaling is the one that works for you.

Authors write a great deal, and the Butt In Chair, Hands On Keyboard (BICHOK) mentality many writers maintain can cause stress by itself. But journaling and creative writing use different kinds of energy. The well you pull from for your character development or story structure differs from the one you access to delve into your personal experiences and reactions. Even for memoir writers, for whom these two might seem similar, the ability to write without an audience can be freeing and take you in different directions than traditional storytelling. Journaling can also be a place to brainstorm, sketch, make a mess with storyboards, and capture ideas. It can be a space to let your mind explore beyond what you'd put on the page for a reader. While a writing project may bring stress, journaling can lift it.

JOURNALING FOR WRITERS

We all want to have a good, sustainable writing habit, in whatever form is right for us. To create a separate journaling habit as a writer, switch it up. If you usually write on the computer, handwrite, use an app, or choose a different location or notebook to help you differentiate your personal journaling from the creative writing you do for your author business. Set it up like any other habit: make a chart, put the pen and notebook on your nightstand, tell friends or family for accountability, and make your plan. Are you working through a book of prompts, making visual art, or free writing? The standardized expressive journal therapy involves three to five sessions over four days, according to the VA, but each person should adjust depending on their plans. Following your own needs and reactions will help you stay consistent and learn what will give you the best results.

If you are looking for simple stress relief and creativity priming, you might choose a fun notebook, some colorful pens, and a bright roll of washi tape, and go to work on a blank page without a prompt. Or maybe you want to focus on a theme and decide to write about how, for example, your favorite story trope has played a role in your own life story.

If you are interested in delving into your emotions and cognitions around a specific incident, you might follow a more structured expressive journaling practice, being careful to give yourself time and mental space for aftercare. Reach out to a professional if it seems helpful, especially if your focus is traumatic or you need more guidance.

All are valid ways to journal, and all have a place in a writer's toolkit. You can start one way and move to another as you find your flow, or dedicate a week or a month to a more difficult process that you want to address, then allow time before and after that is less structured. You could choose to focus on painting while your mind goes free or make a brain-dump list that you'll deal with later. Maybe you brainstorm all the perfect names for a fantasy world, or you write about an author you admire and what made you admire them. In any situation, if your chosen method feels overwhelming or difficult to maintain, recognize that you can take a break or stop completely and move on to something else. Nothing is set in stone, and everything depends on serving you and your process. It will not be perfect, but don't let that hold you back.

Many writers have prepared for journaling with a shelf of lovely, but blank, notebooks. Now is the time to use one or more. Try building a habit, concentrating on development, and enjoying the process.

And as always, progress over perfection, friends. ▪

Jen B. Green

Spend Money to Make Money

I have spoken about marketing many times at conferences, and one subject always gets discussed: money.

Most of the authors I meet don't have a lot of it to throw around, and when they run a few ads and see their hard-earned cash vanish without generating any sales, it makes them not want to spend any more.

This is a paradox. If you don't spend money on ads, you are unlikely to sell any books to generate the money to spend on the ads. It's a chicken-and-egg situation.

So how do you overcome it?

My advice is to learn all you can before you start running ads. Read books and watch online tutorials. Talk to fellow authors who are running ads and see what has worked for them. Reach out to authors in your genre and ask them what audiences they have used successfully, and look at images people are using for their ads.

You can also try browsing the Facebook Ad Library: https://facebook.com/ads/library. Type a genre into the search bar to see what other advertisers are doing.

But let's look further into the future. If you advance to where you have some money set aside and feel confident you can craft an ad and construct an audience, then set a low daily rate and run that ad.

But you can't run just one.

Why not? Because after a million dollars spent on Facebook Ads and six years of testing, I can promise you it is more or less impossible to know what image will resonate with your audience. Typically, I test four to ten images at a time. That's four to ten ads, all with the same copy but using different images. (Remember, it is the image that stops people scrolling. Provided you have aimed at the right audience, your copy and headline should pull them in further, but the image is key.)

Figure 1 is from my Facebook Ads account.

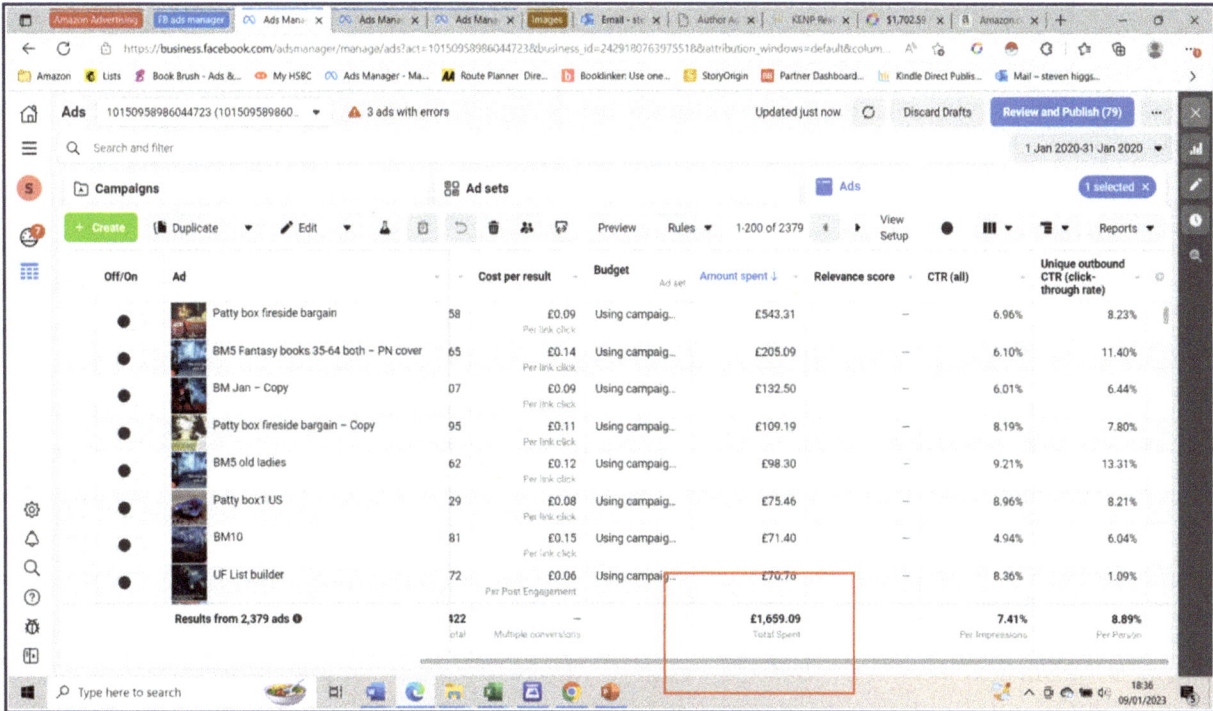

Figure 1

The total spend for the month of January 2020 was roughly $2,000. I sold about $10,000 worth of books—a fairly healthy return, and I made $8,000 profit.

By May of that year, I was spending significantly more—a little more than $6,500, as shown in figure 2.

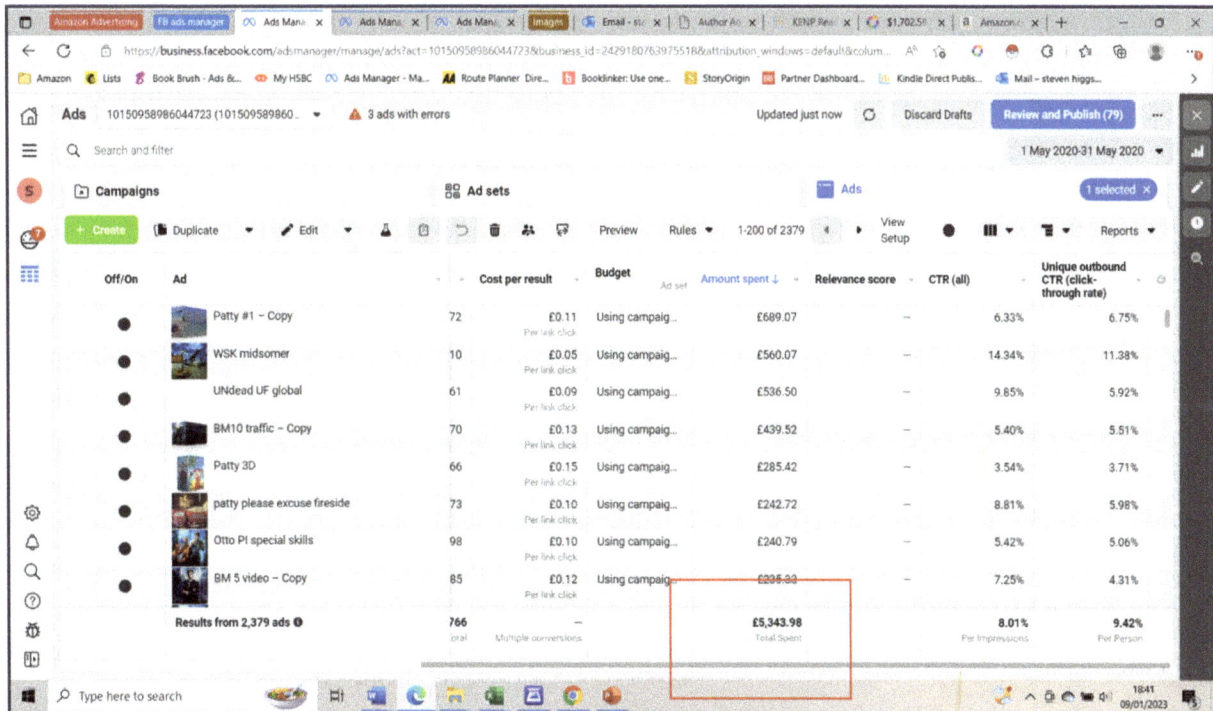

Figure 2

My spending had increased fourfold. However, as shown in figure 3, so had my income.

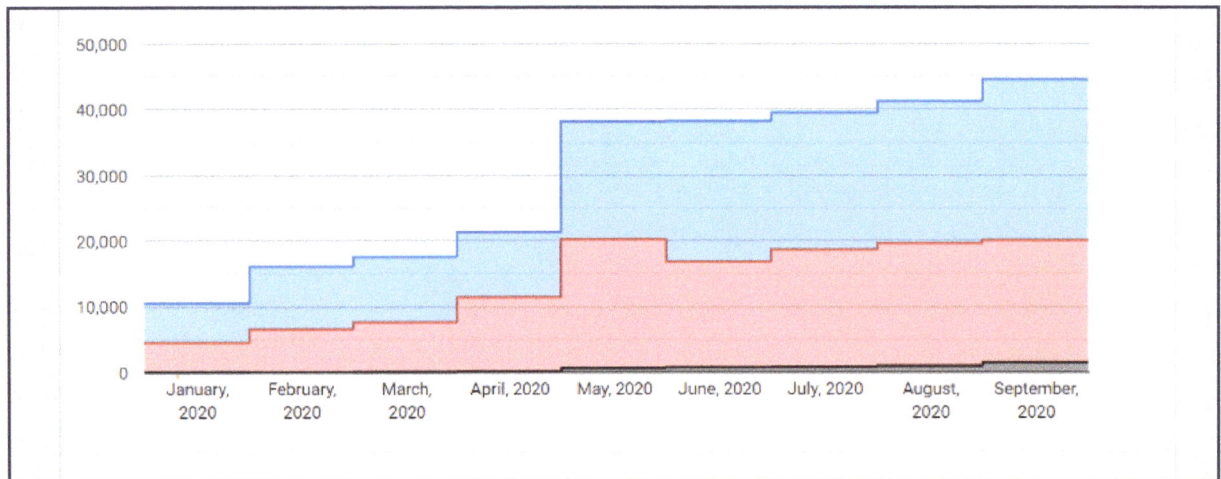

Figure 3

Between January and April 2020, my income went from $10,000 to almost $40,000. Did I suddenly have four times as many books for sale?

No. I marketed the books I had, found ads that worked, and scaled the spending on those ads to generate additional income.

I spent money to make money.

As income from my books had started to trickle in more than a year before this time frame, I'd constantly channeled it back into the next month's ads, always reinvesting a portion of my profit to cover the increasing budget. This minimized the risk of scaling up.

I'm still scaling up now, looking for how I can spend more to make more from the books I have already written.

So if you have a good ad, how much do you increase the budget?

Here's what I do. I run a bunch of ads—four to ten, as I said earlier. The one or two that perform best get to live, and the rest are turned off. Those that remain will have their budgets increased according to how I feel they might perform. This isn't guesswork. It used to be, but thanks to Amazon Attribution links, I can now see whether certain ads are successful. I will double the spend to see if the ad continues to sell books. I will double it again if it continues to work.

Ads will burn out eventually, but you can sell a bunch of books before they do, and through experimentation, you can have new ads up and taking over before your sales dwindle.

Spending $100, $200, or $500 a day might sound scary, but you get to build up to it. All the while, you will be making profit, so what do you care how much you spend?

Now go get those sales! ∎

Steve Higgs

PLANNING TRAVEL TO A CONFERENCE?

Use miles.

Explore ways to make the
most of your award miles.

Writelink.to/unitedair

In This Issue

Executive Team

Chelle Honiker, Publisher

As the publisher of Indie Author Magazine, Chelle Honiker brings nearly three decades of startup, technology, training, and executive leadership experience to the role. She's a serial entrepreneur, founding and selling multiple successful companies including a training development company, travel agency, website design and hosting firm, a digital marketing consultancy, and a wedding planning firm. She's organized and curated multiple TEDx events and hired to assist other nonprofit organizations as a fractional executive, including The Travel Institute and The Freelance Association.

As a writer, speaker, and trainer she believes in the power of words and their ability to heal, inspire, incite, and motivate. Her greatest inspiration is her daughters, Kelsea and Cathryn, who tolerate her tendency to run away from home to play with her friends around the world for months at a time. It's said she could run a small country with just the contents of her backpack.

Alice Briggs, Creative Director

As the creative director of Indie Author Magazine, Alice Briggs utilizes her more than three decades of artistic exploration and expression, business startup adventures, and leadership skills. A serial entrepreneur, she has started several successful businesses. She brings her experience in creative direction, magazine layout and design, and graphic design in and outside of the indie author community to her role.

With a masters of science in Occupational Therapy, she has a broad skill set and uses it to assist others in achieving their desired goals. As a writer, teacher, healer, and artist, she loves to see people accomplish all they desire. She's excited to see how IAM will encourage many authors to succeed in whatever way they choose. She hopes to meet many of you in various places around the world once her passport is back in use.

Nicole Schroeder, Editor in Chief

Nicole Schroeder is a storyteller at heart. As the editor in chief of Indie Author Magazine, she brings nearly a decade of journalism and editorial experience to the publication, delighting in any opportunity to tell true stories and help others do the same. She holds a bachelor's degree from the Missouri School of Journalism and minors in English and Spanish. Her previous work includes editorial roles at local publications, and she's helped edit and produce numerous fiction and nonfiction books, including a Holocaust survivor's memoir, alongside independent publishers. Her own creative writing has been published in national literary magazines. When she's not at her writing desk, Nicole is usually in the saddle, cuddling her guinea pigs, or spending time with family. She loves any excuse to talk about Marvel movies and considers National Novel Writing Month its own holiday.

Monthly Columnists

Honorée Corder

Honorée Corder is the author of more than fifty books, an empire builder, and encourager of writers. When she's not writing, she's spoiling her dog and two cats, eating something fabulous her husband made on the grill, working out, or reading. She hopes this article made a positive impact on your life, and if it did, you'll reach out to her via HonoreeCorder.com.

Craig Martelle

High school Valedictorian enlists in the Marine Corps under a guaranteed tank contract. An inauspicious start that was quickly superseded by excelling in language study. Contract waived, a year at the Defense Language Institute to learn Russian and off to keep my ears on the big red machine during the Soviet years. Earned a four-year degree in two years by majoring in Russian Language. My general staff. career included choice side gigs – UAE, Bahrain, Korea, Russia, and Ukraine.

Major Martelle. I retired from the Marines after a couple years at the embassy in Moscow working arms control issues.

Department of Homeland Security then law school next. I was working for a high-end consulting firm performing business diagnostics, business law, and leadership coaching. For the money they paid me, I was good with that. Just until I wasn't. Then I started writing.

Steve Higgs

High school Valedictorian enlists in the Marine Corps under a guaranteed tank contract. An inauspicious start that was quickly superseded by excelling in language study.

Writers

Heather Clement Davis

Heather Clement Davis has twenty-six years' experience in museums, archaeology, art, counseling, art therapy, creative writing, and nonprofit management. She holds enough graduate work to make a Ph.D. cry as her neurodivergent brain is hooked on learning everything. She's currently a masters candidate in Arts Management. Her paintings and pottery are in galleries and collections worldwide and her poetry and her nonfiction and fiction has found its way to literary journals around the U.S. When not writing or making art, Heather can be found playing Catan or watching Star Trek with her family.

Jen B. Green

Jen B. Green has lived in five countries on four continents with her three sons, two daughters, and one great guy. She reads anything that stays still long enough, plays piano, and bakes everything sweet.

After earning her Ph.D. in psychology, Jen tried writing a novel for Nanowrimo and was hooked! Her days are spent traveling the world, teaching undergraduate psychology, and wrangling her growing homemade army, but her nights are for writing Urban Fantasy with witches and werewolves.

Jenn Lessmann

Jenn Lessmann is the author of three stories published on Amazon's Kindle Vella, two unpublished novels, and a blog that tests Pinterest hacks in the real world (where supplies are sometimes limited, and all projects are overseen by children with digital attention spans). A former barista, stage manager, and high school English teacher with advanced degrees from impressive colleges, she continues to drink excessive amounts of caffeine, stay up later than is absolutely necessary, and read three or four books at a time. She loves lists and the rule of three. Irony too. Jenn is currently studying witchcraft and the craft of writing, and giggling internally whenever they intersect. She writes snarky (not spicy) paranormal fantasy for new adults whenever her dog will allow it.

Merri Maywether

Merri Maywether lives with her husband in rural Montana. You can find her in the town's only coffee house listening to three generations of Montanans share their stories. Otherwise, she's in the classroom or the school library, inspiring the next generation's writers.

Tanya Nellestein

Tanya Nellestein is an avid reader, experience enthusiast, outstanding car vocalist, and Queen of fancy dress. In her spare time she is also a bestselling and award-winning author and journalist with a penchant for bloodthirsty battles and steamy romance. From Vikings to present day, Tanya writes page-turning, gut-churning stories with a romantic angle that always includes good sex

and a happily ever after - eventually. Her debut novel, The Valkyrie's Viking recently hit Amazon's best seller list and her sixth novel, This Side of Fate, was the 2022 winner of the Romance Writers of Australia Sapphire Award for Best Unpublished Romance Manuscript. In 2021, Tanya won the Romance Writers of Australia Romance in Media Award. Tanya lives on the outskirts of Sydney, Australia amidst a cavalcade of never ending disasters, both natural and those of her own making.

Eryka Parker

Eryka Parker is a book coach, an award-winning developmental editor, and writing instructor. As a women's contemporary author under the pen name Zariah L. Banks, she creates emotional intimacy novels that prove that everyone deserves to feel seen, appreciated, and loved. She lives in Northeast Ohio with her husband and two children and is currently working on her third novel.

Tiffany Robinson

Tiffany Robinson writes contemporary romance under two different pen names because she loves the happily-ever-after. She's also a freelance content writer, writing coach, and online educator. She and her husband have been running their own business since 2010 and have two young boys who keep them on their toes. Prior to marriage, children, and an online career, Tiffany was employed in the field of Exercise Science and Injury Rehabilitation. That experience taught her that communication styles are as wide and varied as East is to West (East and West never touch...), and that makes it a beautiful thing when common ground and common interests are found. Outside of writing, running a business, and momming, her hobbies include cooking and running. She knows it's weird, but everybody's got their thing.

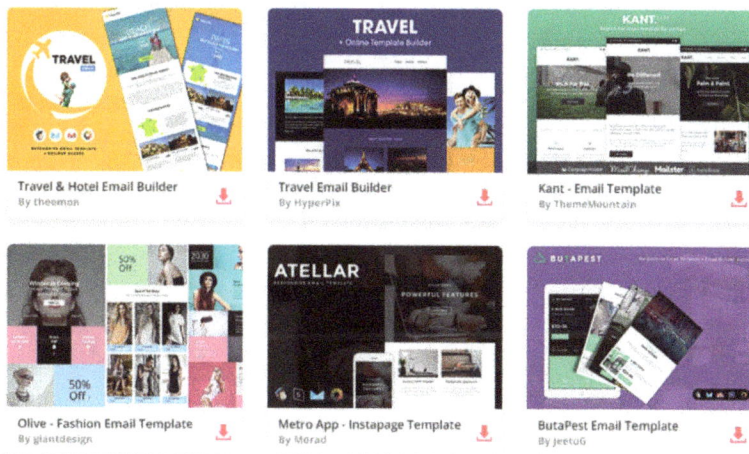

PUBLISHER ROCKET

FIND
PROFITABLE
KINDLE
KEYWORDS
Book Marketing Research
Made Simple!

writelink.to/pubrocket